Hoover Dam

ABDO Publishing Company

A Buddy Book
by
Julie Murray

VISIT US AT
www.abdopub.com

Published by ABDO Publishing Company, 4940 Viking Drive, Edina, Minnesota 55435.

Copyright © 2005 by Abdo Consulting Group, Inc. International copyrights reserved in all countries. No part of this book may be reproduced in any form without written permission from the publisher. Buddy Books™ is a trademark and logo of ABDO Publishing Company.

Printed in the United States.

Edited by: Christy DeVillier
Contributing Editors: Michael P. Goecke, Sarah Tieck
Graphic Design: Deborah Coldiron
Image Research: Deborah Coldiron
Photographs: Corbis, Hulton Archives, Photodisc

Library of Congress Cataloging-in-Publication Data

Murray, Julie, 1969-
  Hoover Dam / Julie Murray.
    p. cm. — (All aboard America)
  Includes index.
  Summary: A brief history of Hoover Dam, considered to be one of seven modern civil engineering wonders in America.
  ISBN 1-59197-506-9
    1. Hoover Dam (Ariz. and Nev.)—History—Juvenile literature. [1. Hoover Dam (Ariz. and Nev.)] I. Title.

TC557.5.H6M87 2003
627'.82'0979313—dc21

                                             2003050308

Table of Contents

The Hoover Dam 4

The Colorado River 6

Building The Dam 8

The Workers 12

The Finished Dam 15

The Power Plant 17

The Hoover Dam Today 19

Fun Facts 21

Important Words 22

Web Sites 23

Index 24

The Hoover Dam

The Hoover Dam is one of the largest dams ever built. It is 1,244 feet (379 m) long and 726 feet (221 m) tall. That is three times as tall as the Statue of Liberty.

A dam stands on a stream or river and controls the water's flow. The Hoover Dam controls the wild waters of the Colorado River. It is in Black Canyon on the border of Nevada and Arizona. The Hoover Dam also has a power plant that produces electricity.

It took five years to build the Hoover Dam (HOO-ver DAM).

The Colorado River

The Colorado River is 1,450 miles (2,334 km) long. It begins in Colorado's Rocky Mountains and flows southwest. It goes through the Grand Canyon and ends at the Gulf of California.

People have depended on the Colorado River for a long time. They have used its water for drinking and for watering crops. Sometimes the Colorado River overflowed and caused floods. These floods damaged homes and farmland.

Seven states use water from the Colorado River.

A dam would put an end to floods. It would allow people to use the water all the time. So in 1928, Congress agreed to build a Colorado River dam. The Bureau of Reclamation was in charge of the project. They hired a company named Six Companies to build it.

Building The Dam

Six Companies began working on the Hoover Dam project in 1931. First, it removed loose rock from the canyon walls. This work was done by high-scalers. High-scalers climbed down the canyon walls using ropes. They used **jackhammers** and **dynamite** to remove loose rock.

Removing river water from the building site was the next step. Workers dug two large tunnels on each side of the canyon. They also built two **cofferdams**. The cofferdams forced the river water into the tunnels. This helped to keep the building site free of water.

More than five million tons (4,535,900 t) of concrete make up the Hoover Dam.

On June 6, 1933, workers began building the Hoover Dam. They poured concrete into hundreds of columns. The columns were different sizes. Some were about 60 feet (18 m) wide. Workers used **grout** to hold the concrete columns together.

Detour ⬇

Did You Know?

At one time, the Hoover Dam was called the Boulder Dam. In 1947, the name changed to the Hoover Dam. The dam was named after President Herbert Hoover, the 31st president of the United States.

President Herbert Hoover

The Workers

Many Americans did not have jobs in 1931. This time in history is called the Great Depression. People moved across the country to get jobs working on the Hoover Dam.

The Hoover Dam was built during the Great Depression.

More than 5,000 people worked on the Hoover Dam. At first, workers and their families lived in camps called Ragtowns. They had no electricity or water. Later, the U.S. government built Boulder City for the workers. Boulder City had houses, streets, stores, and electricity. Only the Hoover Dam workers could live there.

The Hoover Dam project gave jobs to thousands of people.

Building the Hoover Dam was hard work. People worked seven days a week. They worked on hot, 120-degree-Fahrenheit (49°C) summer days. Some workers faced danger every day. Ninety-six people died building the Hoover Dam.

The Finished Dam

The Hoover Dam was finished in May 1935. The project was done two years earlier than expected. President Franklin D. Roosevelt honored the Hoover Dam on September 30, 1935. He called it "another great achievement of American resourcefulness, skill, and determination."

President Franklin D. Roosevelt

Extra water from the Colorado River became Lake Mead. Lake Mead is the Hoover Dam's **reservoir**. Millions of people use water from the reservoir every day.

Lake Mead is the largest man-made lake in the United States. It has 550 miles (885 km) of shoreline. In some places, Lake Mead is 500 feet (152 m) deep. Many people use the lake for water sports.

The Power Plant

The Hoover Dam power plant has been working since 1936. It uses the river's force to make electricity. This power plant makes enough electricity to light 500,000 homes.

Turbines help produce electricity at the Hoover Dam power plant.

The Hoover Dam has four intake towers. They are each 395 feet (120 m) tall. These intake towers control the power plant's water supply. Water flows from the towers through large pipes. These pipes go underground to the **turbines**. The turbines turn 17 **generators** that produce electricity.

The Hoover Dam's water intake towers

The Hoover Dam Today

An old turbine on display at the Hoover Dam Visitor Center.

People have been touring the Hoover Dam since 1937. Visitors can take the Discovery Tour. It features many displays and presentations. An observation deck offers great views of Lake Mead and the Colorado River. People can visit the power plant, too.

Highway 93 takes people across the Hoover Dam.

Visitors can drive across the Hoover Dam on Highway 93. Thousands of people go across it each day. One million people visit the Hoover Dam each year.

Detour

Fun Facts:

- Hoover Dam spans 1,244 feet (379 m) across the Black Canyon.
- The Hoover Dam's base is 660 feet (201 m) thick.
- It cost $175 million to build the Hoover Dam.
- The Hoover Dam is as tall as a 72-story building.
- There is enough concrete in the Hoover Dam to build a two-lane highway from San Francisco, California to New York, New York.
- The Hoover Dam weighs 6,600,000 tons (5,987,419 t).

Important Words

cofferdam (KAW-fuhr-dam) a special wall-like structure that allows water to be pumped out of an area.

dynamite (DY-nuh-might) used for blowing up, or exploding, things.

generator (JEH-nuh-ray-tuhr) a machine that changes energy into electricity.

grout (GROWT) a special mixture that holds together concrete and other materials.

jackhammer (JAK-ham-mer) a tool for drilling rock.

reservoir (REH-zuh-vwar) a place for collecting and storing water.

turbine (TER-byn) an engine driven by water.

Web Sites

Would you like to learn more about the Hoover Dam?

Please visit ABDO Publishing Company on the information superhighway to find Web site links about the Hoover Dam. These links are routinely monitored and updated to provide the most current information available.

www.abdopub.com

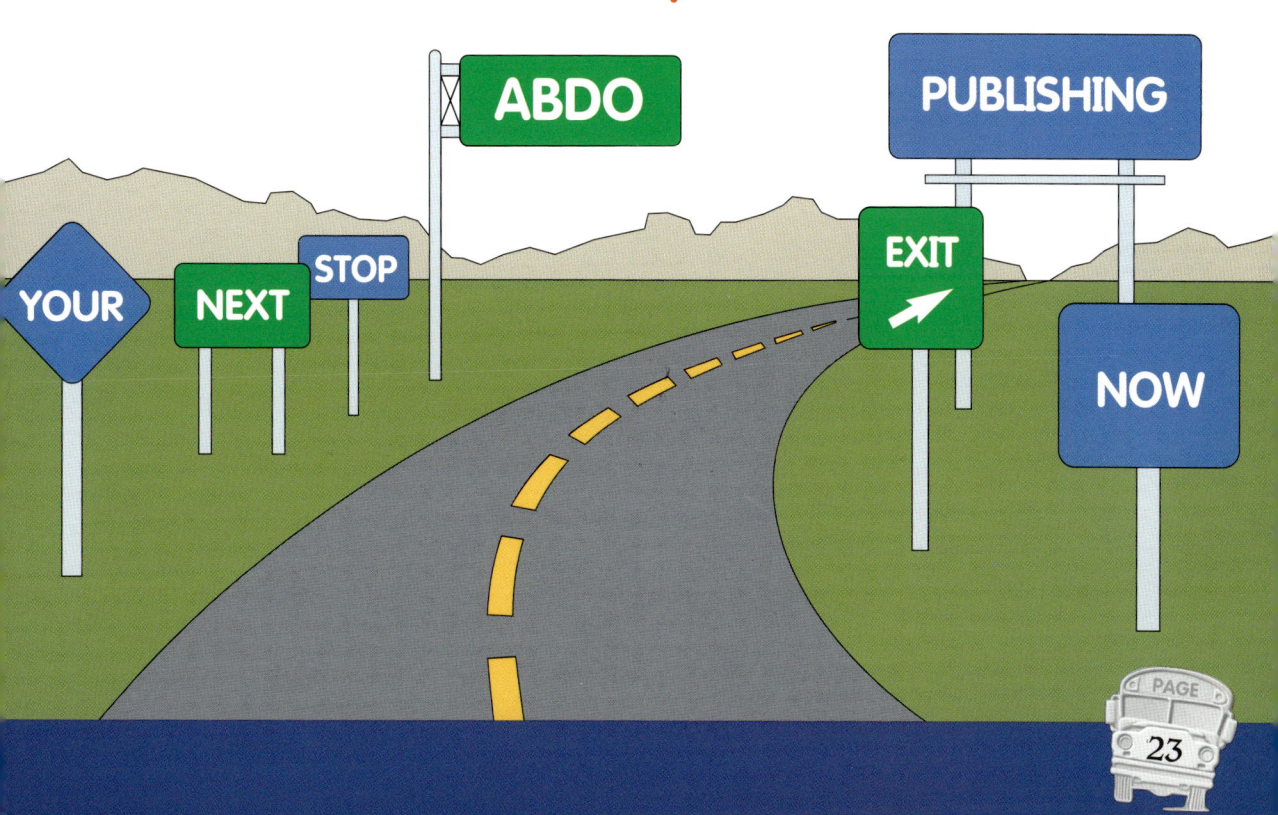

Index

Arizona **4**

Black Canyon **4, 21**

Boulder City **13**

Bureau of Reclamation **7**

California, Gulf of **6**

cofferdams **9**

Colorado **6**

Colorado River **4, 6, 7, 16, 19**

columns **10**

concrete **10, 21**

Discovery Tour **19**

dynamite **8**

electricity **4, 13, 17, 18**

generators **18**

Grand Canyon **6**

Great Depression **12**

high-scalers **8**

Hoover, Herbert **11**

jackhammers **8**

Mead, Lake **16, 19**

Nevada **4**

New York, NY **21**

power plant **4, 17, 18, 19**

Ragtowns **13**

Rocky Mountains **6**

Roosevelt, Franklin D. **15**

San Francisco, CA **21**

Six Companies **7, 8, 9**

Statue of Liberty **4**

tunnels **9**

turbines **17, 18, 19**